Fortune Cookie Wisdom

Fortune Cookie Wisdom

Joseph Quincy Knight

ARPress
ILLUMINATING IDEAS
EMPOWERING VOICES

ARPress
45 Dan Road Suite 5
Canton MA 02021

Hotline:	1(888) 821-0229
Fax:	1(508) 545-7580

Ordering Information:
Quantity sales. Special discounts are available on quantity purchases by corporations, associations, and others. For details, contact the publisher at the address above.

Printed in the United States of America.

ISBN-13:	Paperback	979-8-89330-691-0
	eBook	979-8-89330-690-3

Library of Congress Control Number: 2024901786

Contents

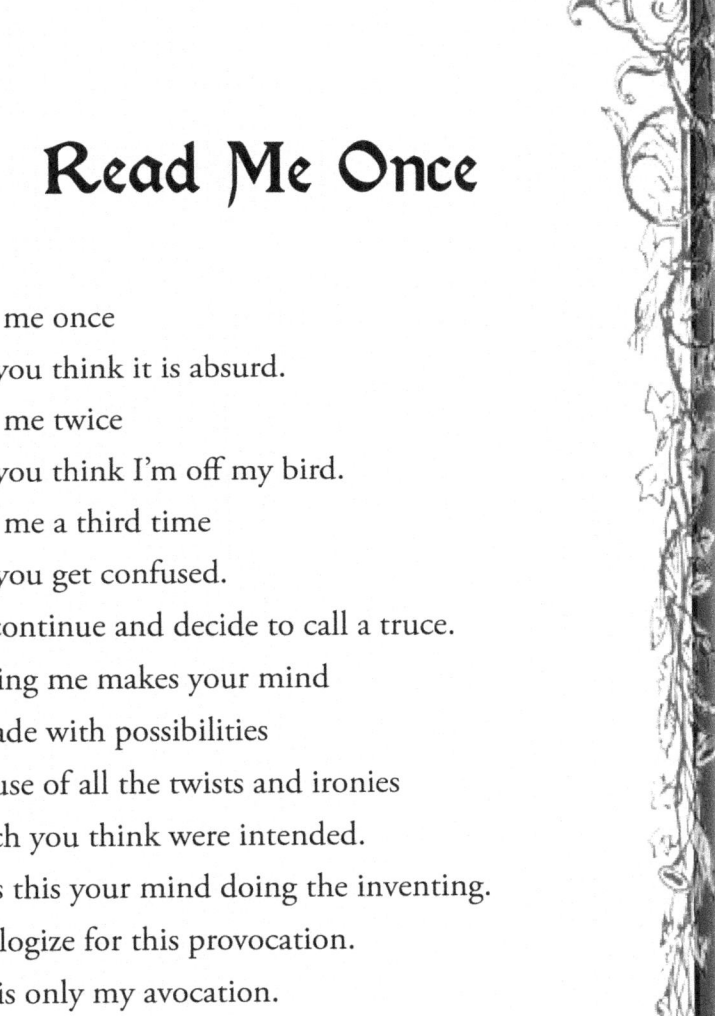

Read Me Once

Read me once

And you think it is absurd.

Read me twice

And you think I'm off my bird.

Read me a third time

And you get confused.

You continue and decide to call a truce.

Reading me makes your mind

Cascade with possibilities

Because of all the twists and ironies

Which you think were intended.

Or, is this your mind doing the inventing.

I apologize for this provocation.

This is only my avocation.

We All Wept for Lisa

It's been forty two years
Since Lisa passed away,
A victim of CF.
She always knew her days were numbered,
So she tried to make the best
Of whatever time she had left.
She set goals for herself
And consistently found practical solutions
And remained clearheaded—never in confusion.
 She briefly enjoyed being a woman
And fell in love
With her high school sweetheart.
They planned to go far away to school
Against Dad's wishes. Then she died.
She left behind her arts and crafts
That we continue to treasure.
I feel her spirit watching over me
When I think of her at my leisure.

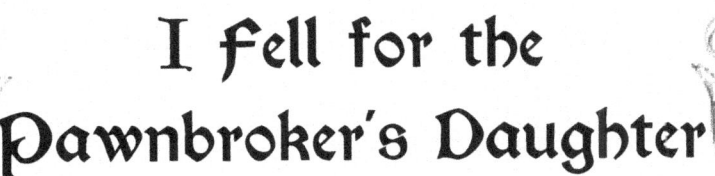

I Fell for the Pawnbroker's Daughter

I fell for the pawnbroker's daughter.
She likes to tidy her place
Keeping things from going out of order.
She learned a few lessons
That Mom and Dad taught her.

After several years
Of love and laughter, I still worry.
She hates to rush into a situation.
No, she doesn't like to hurry.
I gave her the family engagement ring.
 I told her that she means everything.

Still it seems like we'll never marry.
She insists on doubting me
And continues to tarry.
Who knows what our future may bring.
 I sure hope she doesn't
Pawn the family ring.

Have You Ever Seen an Angel?

Have you ever seen an angel?
Can I be yours tonight?
You're such a special lady.
 I plan to treat you right.

Do you believe in heaven?
If it is so, we should both wait
Until we reach a ripe old age.
The Good Book says that it's great.

But in the meantime,
We'll find heaven in each other's arms.
I promise to love you forever
And to cause you no harm.

Have you ever seen an angel?
 It may be no surprise.
When you look in the mirror,
Open your big brown eyes.

How Bright
Is Your Aura?

How bright is your aura?
Can you make me glow?
How warm is your touch?
 You know how I love you so.

How strong is your heart beat
When we come near?
How bright is your aura?
You have nothing to fear.

How much do you love me?
As much as I love you?
Don't forsake me, darling.
Or else, I wouldn't know what to do.

How bright is your aura?
Is it brighter than mine?
I trust you, baby
Because you are honest and so kind.

If I Gave You the Hope Diamond

If I gave you the Hope diamond

Would you treasure it all your life?

Or, would you auction it off at Christies,

And refuse to be my wife?

Like your personality.

A diamond has many facets

Which never fails to bring me delight

Just as a it sparkles

Under the moonlight.

I could get you an opal

Because you are a Libra child,

Would you tarry too long

Making me wait a long long while?

Perhaps you might prefer

The Star of Asia.

Would five hundred carats amaze ya?

If this is still not enough,

I guess it's because money can't buy love.

A Babe on a Budget

She's no spendthrift.
She picks out each gift
With much thought
And everything she has bought
Has a lesson that one should not forget
 About being a babe on a budget.

She wears a colorful dress,
Always looking her best.
She has brown eyes
That help me realize
Whomever becomes her man
Will be her lucky prize.

How fortunate her beau shall be
When he and she come to be.
I plan to remain a good friend
And see her casually.

The Story of Suzanne

Here's the story of Suzanne.
She lives in Paris
And dances the can-can.
Spent her life going
From man to man.
I met up with her.
She gave me a smile.
She was charming for just a while.
Until, the authorities came along.
Then, she sang her sad old song.
I spent six months
Being put away.
All I wanted to do
Was to go out and play
My lucky harmonica
And sing the blues
About how Suzanne and I
 Have to pay our dues.
She means well but is often confused.

A Gal Named Smith

Oh 411, I need information

Because I'm looking for a gal named Smith.

After college, we parted as friends

And I want to send her a little gift.

She became a mother

And I lost my brother.

I got over it and still have fun.

She taught me the chords with no rewards.

I never learned how to strum.

Oh 411, please information

Has she moved real far away?

She must come around

To visit her folks and friends in town.

You see, I've got a few things to say.

We hung out together for four years,

And she said that was too long.

She taught me how to play the "Gambler"

Because that was her favorite song.

I write every night. I'm still going strong.

A Tribute to
My Fellow Travelers

Born with the touch of the poet,

People of all walks of life

Both famous and unknown

Have had their lives disrupted

By a devastating disease which causes the mind

To invent a world to hide in.

People feel bad.

But all-too-often, they shy away.

Many great people in the arts

As well as in all human endeavors

Suffer this chemical imbalance.

I have decided to join a support group

And I learned that many of my problems

Are shared by people just as I.

We all had our lives derailed,

And are finding hope with medication

So that we can set sail

To the life we wish we could have had.

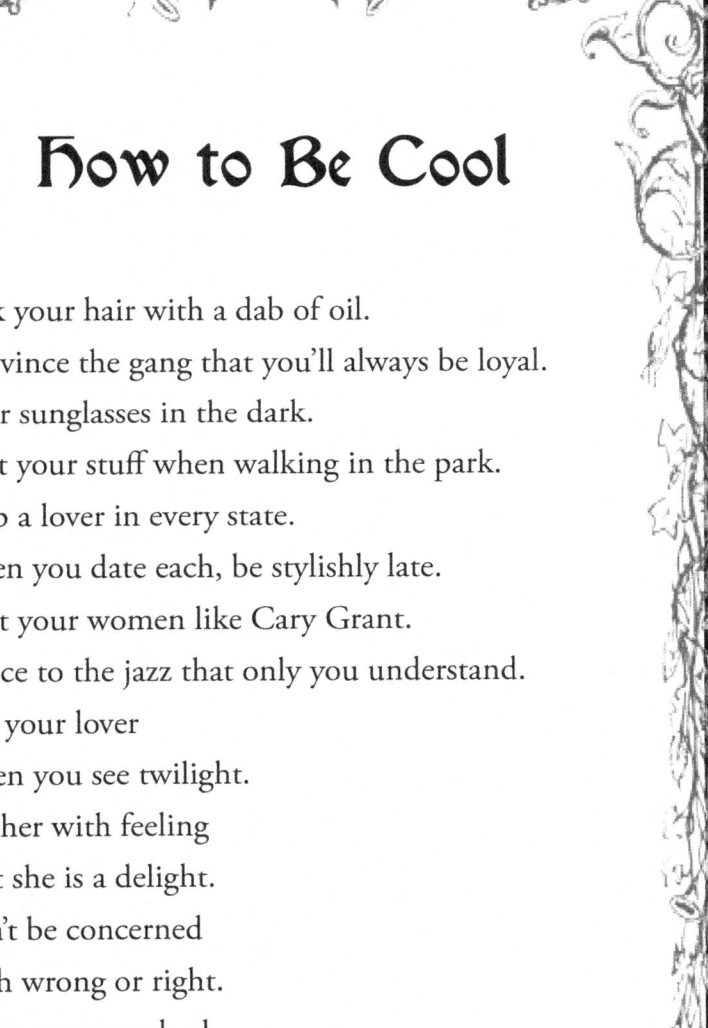

How to Be Cool

Slick your hair with a dab of oil.

Convince the gang that you'll always be loyal.

Wear sunglasses in the dark.

Strut your stuff when walking in the park.

Keep a lover in every state.

When you date each, be stylishly late.

Treat your women like Cary Grant.

Dance to the jazz that only you understand.

Kiss your lover

When you see twilight.

Tell her with feeling

That she is a delight.

Don't be concerned

With wrong or right.

Make sure your bark

Is louder than your bite.

Use those stern eyebrows

Should someone challenge you to a fight.

Keep your lips loose and the wallet tight.

All About This Man of Doubt

This will help you get the gist
With my simple list
That will tell you what I'm all about
This is the story of a man of doubt.
He is an obscure poet, compulsive student,
An over-spender, mental health consumer,
Always late, a late bloomer,
Island fool, soothsayer, private worshipper,
Online prayer, weight watcher,
Confirmed bachelor, mama's boy, black sheep,
Movie addict, tune lover, composer and writer,
Magical thinker, wisdom seeker,
Over-sleeper, saver of the world,
But not himself, chaotic life,
No children nor wife,
Not much money saved but still lucky,
Talks to the dead and invisible friends,
Sometimes touching, other times, touched,
Forgives, forgets and makes amends.

As Far As I'm Concerned

Grass is green.

Daisies are yellow.

I may be a poet

But I'm not a gay fellow.

There are angels in heaven,

Demons in hell.

Will my prayers be answered?

Only time will tell.

If you study hard,

And stay out of trouble,

No one can come along

And burst your bubble.

Whatever subject you take time to learn

Is yours' to keep

As far as I'm concerned.

A Legion of Angels

May a legion of angels,
Fifty thousand strong
Who fear neither evil nor death
March into the eye of the storm.

May legion of angels
Answer each individual's prayer
From the hearts of mothers and their children
And bring them shelter from the storm.

May a legion of angels
From each state in the land
Hold out for the common good
With the Good Lord at their command.

May a legion of angels
Depart back to Heaven
As the rainbow shines
Leaving behind faith in the Divine.

A Clenched Fist

Open your heart.
Open your mind.
If you want the Lord's blessing.
It's not hard to find.

A mind filled with conflicts,
Insecurity and hate
Cannot find the Lord
Before it's too late.

Here is an offer
You can't resist.
Add a little charity
To your shopping list.

When you start to give, you'll start to live.
Drop your defenses and remember this.
The Lord can't
Put his blessing in a clenched fist.

A Mental Housecleaning

First, I'll remove
All the thorns by my side.
Then, I'll mop up all the blood
Dripping from my bleeding heart.
I'll wipe away the frown from my face.
I'll warm up my engines
And rejoin the human race.
I'll open my eyes wide
So that the sun will shine
Into the windows of my mind.
I'll brush off
All the snow from my shoulder peaks.
I'll trim down the shrubbery
That adorns my head.
I'll think of only clean thoughts
So that I can get ahead.
I'll polish my choppers
So that they are as shiny as ceramic tile,
And I'll greet the world with a big sloppy smile.

Behold the Lobster!

This is my mercy plea for lobsters
That have come straight out of the sea
To be displayed in your supermarket's tank
Regardless how deep they had sank.

Yes, they taste great
 When boiled alive
With a little slice of butter on the side.

Still, a sea bug is a sea bug.
You might as well eat a fly.
So next time you go to the supermarket,
Take a good look at one, eye to eye.

Behold the lobster marooned in the tank!
Yes they sure taste good
After walking the plank.

Castles in the Air

For those of you who wish to invent,
But are held back by fear.
Hold on to your dreams
Even if the idea is up in the air.
You should be confident and jolly
No matter if you are accused of folly.
People may insult your rank.
Remember, some day
You could be laughing
All the way to the bank.
Then, the news would spread everywhere
That you dared to dream
Of castles in the air.

Brinkmanship

First, a hostile nation
Draws its line in the sand.
Why are they so combative?
Most of us do not understand.
As they increase their arsenal,
What should any God-fearing nation do?
Threat meets counter-threat,
And pretty soon, we are all living in peril.
We should let the President lose sleep
Over this while we citizens pray for him.
I guess we must live
By the goodness of the hearts
Of our worst enemies.
Kind David in his psalms and Jesus in sermon
Had suggested that we must face our enemies
By dining and conversing with them
Face to face. Soon, we will discover that
Our worst fears are just misunderstandings.

Death of a Playwright

Arthur Miller captured the heart of America
By questioning the American dream.
Of course, he got to marry Marylyn
So he could direct her life, scene by scene.

I remember how in high school,
I tackled "The Crucible"
While learning about McCarthyism
And how every play has its hidden themes.

Although just a kid,
I was glad I tackled his work
Because it helped me to learn and grow
A little more than good old Captain Kirk.

We will never forget Willy Lowman
whose broken life was shared by all.
You see those who aim too high,
Risk taking the big fall.

Digital Dreams

After a hard day of rocking and rolling

Through the streets of the city,

Chasing buses and trains

To make an appointment

That was later cancelled

Leaving me extra time

To run to the bookstore

And read up on digital photography

Over a cup of coffee

Trying not to spill it, or else

End up paying for the manual.

It was a half-hour read

And I am now fully enlightened.

You see that I am totally equipped

To pick out the correct mega pixels

And paint the most vivid digital dream

That the mind's eye could ever imagine.

All I need is a puppy and my girl, Bonny

To pose for me. (Don't be modest.)

Fortune Favors the Bold

It doesn't matter
Whether you are young or old.
If you want to find your pot of gold,
The same old lesson has to be told.
Fortune favors the bold.
There was Caesar, Charlemagne
And Judah the Maccabee
Who all used their faith
To help them achieve their destiny.
There was Washington, Jefferson
And don't forget Honest Abe.
Who stood firm in conflict
And they proudly remained brave.
So let me repeat myself
If you don't mind being once more told.
If you want your dream to come true,
Fortune favors the bold.

Going for the Small Victory

Some say it's all or nothing.

But, that is not really true.

You do the best that you can

And somehow you'll get through

A life full of obstructions

And thorns upon your side.

But keep smiling

And you may be admiring

Those who came along for the ride.

When you know you have a weakness,

You shouldn't be afraid

To try to work around it.

Don't let anyone tell you

That you are unfit to make a living.

An old friend left these dying words

To me in a dream.

Just keep on struggling For those small victories

And you'll always be on your team.

Gravity

I would float away
Into the heavens
With my dreams being supported
By my open wings.
But gravity pulls me down
So that I remain
With my feet fixed on the ground.
Yes, this is holiday time.
I would like to celebrate.
Still, looking at my bank statement
Makes me want to hesitate.
Eventually, like a dagger to the gut,
I shall feel
The gravity of my situation.
I should not panic.
It's only money.
I must undergo a financial operation
To match my liabilities
With my assets and find a way to pay
My creditors who keep on asking.

Hello, Mr. Scale.

Hello, Mr. Scale

Don't tell me the same old tale

About my big appetite

Which is why my jeans are tight.

Yes, it is a deadly fight

And I must do what is right

To cut back—bite by bite

Until my love-handles are out of sight.

When my friend, the doc,

Who has been my savior and rock,

Advises me

To lose a few pounds,

I might be able

To avoid a couple rounds

Of steak and cheese cake

And all those goodies that I like

And visit the park

To take a long hike.

Henry VIII Armor

In his later years,
Henry VIII was fitted with
A fine coat of armor
Which now is on display
At the Metropolitan Museum.
Henry and I are both husky and require a XXL.
It definitely looks like my size.
I could probably use Henry's suit of armor
When I go back into active duty
In the piers or container fields.
Or possibly during a foreign inspection
In Iraq,
Or perhaps during a return to Israel,
I could wear Henry's regalia
When touring the West Bank
Or hitch-hiking through the Gaza strip.
I think any suicide bomber
Would wet his pants laughing
Before getting a chance to blow himself up.

I Am Not Incompetent

Challenged by complex feelings
That cause me to lose touch with reality.
With altered paranoid perceptions,
I am lost when chemical imbalances
Cause me to imagine the worst
And evil conspiracies lurk everywhere.
My trusted friends and family members
Come under suspicion.
Then, after spending time in the hospital,
The sunshine returns and I apologize
After going into hiding and disappearing
From the real world.
Fortunately, I can return to work.
However, it should be pointed out that
As lucky as I am to still have a job,
I am not incompetent.
I am just impaired.
I still deserve to have a life!

I Am Writing This Requiem for Myself

Thus said Mozart
As that dark figure went past his door
While Mozart continued composing
Knowing that his days were numbered.
Not having Constanza to comfort him
With only a pretty melody
In his head to raise his spirits,
He was exhausted, unwell and completely bankrupt
Owing money to all his friends and admirers.
What Mozart failed to realize
Was that while his own life was to be brief,
His music shall live forever.
So as we celebrate
The 267th birthday of the most gifted,
Temperamental musical genius who ever lived,
We continue to be mesmerized by the magic of Mozart
When we visit our concert halls.
To his period's Zeitgeist
Shall be with us as long as music exists.

Spending Man

I'm a spending man
Without a spending plan.
This is why
I like to live off the land.
With my lucky credit card
I charge whenever I get the urge in my heart,
I don't hesitate to part
With other people's money in trust of God.

I am a spending man.
So get out of my way.
I'm in a hurry to buy
But the payback will have to be delayed.

I am a spending man.
Watch out Mr. Equifax.
Just be cool and try to relax.
You see, I am expecting a lottery win.
Or else, I am waiting for my boat to come in.

If You Think It Is So?

I eat, drink and breathe;
Therefore, I live.
I live; therefore, I exist.
I exist; therefore, I think.
"I think, therefore I am," says Descartes.
"I am what I am," says the musical.
"This does not mean I am gay," say I.
However, I live for love.
I couldn't love you
If I didn't love myself.
If we broke up, we'd still live
(unless we were Romeo and Juliet).
If we live, we could still exist apart.
"To be or not to be," as Hamlet says.
If we chose to be apart,
We could exist, live and love
As well as we did together.
This is so if you think it is so?

If It Were My Son

What if it were my son

When they come knocking at my door?

How will I know how to respond

On the gloomiest day in April

When we'd get the news from the Pentagon

Of how my son paid the ultimate price

To serve his country with valor?

I could never speak with him again

Because he is now with a higher power.

While in Rome,

Do as the Romans do.

But there are times

When this tragedy happens to you,

The voice of dissent rings true.

London or Paris

Is it dogs or cats you prefer?

Do you like hair or fur?

Would you like a tomato or a potato?

Or how about a tommato or a potatto?

Is it wine or beer

That you use to wish a good cheer?

Do you do your chores now or later?

Is your generosity lesser or greater?

Are you arrogant or humble?

Do you speak clearly or mumble?

If you could make only one desert getaway,

Would you visit Vegas or Jerusalem?

Would you choose

Between the Lady Luck or the Lord?

Does saying a prayer make you bored?

If you had to travel to Europe,

Would it be London or Paris?

When you go home,

Would saying au revior make you embarrassed?

Living in a House of Cards

I am living in a house of cards.

The higher my debts grow,

The sooner my house will collapse.

This will leave me

To pitch a tent

On the side of the road

Because if this trend continues,

I won't be able to afford my rent.

I also consult the good ole tarot deck

Which is the omen of my good fortune

And makes me prognosticate.

I hope that the stars

Shine in my constellation.

So my astrologer can affirm

That in this new year,

I really have nothing to fear.

I hope I am no longer

At the mercy of the gods

And have been dealt a few lucky cards.

Must Artists Compete?

Must every artistic feat

Be rewarded as if one has to compete?

I know that human nature

Makes every transaction a race.

However, reward statues tarnish

And so does the artist's grace.

In art, one takes a self-defined test

To bring out one's personal best.

The money a work of art earns

Belongs to the public

As far as I am concerned.

Whether he or she is painting a sunset,

Rhyming a couplet,

Or penning an opera's libretto,

All an artist needs is his daily bread

And a modest loft in the ghetto

Where he can make people see darkness

Or joyfully celebrate

A portrayal of life in all its starkness.

On Martyrdom

Many great leaders
Choose martyrdom to prove to the world
That they are sincere
About their beliefs.
However, there has never been a single case
When a simple apology,
Rephrasing or compromise
Could result in being forgiven
By the believer's adversary.
It is a great misdeed
To deliberately end one's life
And a bigger shame
To take others along with you
For the sake of a cause
Be it religious or political.
Effort is the only way to promote beliefs
By passing on values face to face
Without mortifying the flesh.
The road to salvation is an arduous struggle
To live in the world you help save.

Parallel Lives Caught in Forbidden Love

Two of the most beautiful
And intelligent woman in history
Led parallel lives
Because each pursued forbidden love.
The woman who stole David's heart
Did so to cheer him up
After David suffered
His most devastating defeat.
However, to get his true love,
David had to mortally betray a good friend.
A similar tragedy occurred
Under different circumstances
When Cleopatra seduced Marc Anthony.
Bathsheba and Cleopatra paid dearly
For their romances with controversies
And terrible tragedies to each.
Both women lived under the same karma.
Neither woman will ever be forgotten.

Seven

There are seven days of Creation.

On the seventh day, the Holy Land rested.

There are seven days in a week,

On the Sabbath, we rest and worship.

There are thirty seven trillion cells

In the human body

Which get replenished every seven years.

Catholics believe in seven deadly sins.

Muslims believe in seven heavens

Including the atmosphere, shooting stars,

The meteoroids, the moon, planets,

comets and the sun.

This is why Jewish people

Consider seven a lucky number.

Joseph-Ism

Belief that one can converse with the deity.

Belief that there are other deities

And civilizations throughout the universe.

Belief that the Lord

Can show you a sign

To alter your perceptions no matter the cost

Should He feels the matter is that important.

Belief that sticking to one's convictions

Can cause one's ideas to be spread

Without the necessity to publish.

Because Heaven can be used creatively.

The notion that there should be

Equality of all the major faiths.

The supernatural

Is only the natural unexplained.

If you are reverent and observant,

God will treat you with mercy.

Belief in reincarnation and channeling.

Tale of Two Tall Towers

There once were two tall towers

That stood in our great city.

Some thought they were ugly,

Others thought they were pretty.

They became our national symbol,

Some say of greatness; others, great excess.

Then, the terrorists struck

And made a horrifying mess.

We must now remember the victims

Who were busy at another day of work.

While struggling to escape,

They left behind a few last words

Such as, "Tell the children I love them,"

And, "I am trapped and can't get out."

The firemen sang and joked

While trying not to cry out loud.

Yes, 9/11 was our wake-up call,

The day America had its back against the wall.

The Case of the Divinizing Detective

There once was a divinizing detective
Whose sleuthing was quite selective.
When he gets a call,
He looks into his crystal ball
And chooses his best elective.
When the first clue arrives,
He opens his eyes
And follows his prime directive.
He pursues his chase
With reckless abandon and haste.
When frustrated, he might cite an invective.
He always gets his man
Whether by sea or on land
Because he is
The undaunted divinizing detective.

The Day the House of Words Tumbled Down

It doesn't matter
Whether you smile or frown
When recalling the day
The House of Words tumbled down.

The subjects rebelled
Against their predicates.
The plurals went singular.
Adverbs ceased to modify.
The various parts of speech went speechless.

Pronouns no longer agreed.
All diction was rude.
English teachers engaged in a big feud.

Shakespeare was driven to tears.
What does any advocate of proper
English do?
The day the House of Words tumbled down,
Everyone babbled that we were through.

The Four Options

God turned to Metastophocles

When He was about to end the world.

Being the Merciful One,

He first asked what His options are.

Metastophocles answered with a silly grin,

"You can travel back into the past.

You can travel into the future.

You can go into outer space

Or you can join me in the Nether-regions."

Both of them laughed.

"I'll tell you where I would like to go.

I think I'll let the world keep turning

on its own while I head off

to the retirement home

for gods and goddesses.

Despite all the advantages

I have given Mankind, they will never learn.

The more advanced they get,

The more certain they are that I am dead."

The Hamster and the Snake

Here is a tale

Not to be believed.

It shows that there is goodness

Even among snakes.

When offered a hamster

For a daily meal,

The snake showed mercy

And let the hamster crawl up and down his back.

So, the snake decided not to attack.

For several months,

The two have become friends.

Who knows how this relationship ends.

The Trinity

There is a trinity
That exists in America
Making this a great land of freedom.

In order to have freedom,
One needs to have virtue.
Virtue makes one respect his neighbor
As he wants to be respected.

In order to have virtue,
One has to have faith.
Faith in our country.
Faith in one's family.
And if you so choose,
Faith in God.

Faith, virtue and freedom
Are a powerful combination
That enables us to pursue happiness
With liberty.

There Is a Cosmic Symphony

There is a cosmic symphony
Emanating from the very fabric
Of time and space.
There is a cosmic symphony
Which came to be in a giant energy wave
Helped by God's good grace.
From the time of the Big Bang
Over fourteen billion years ago.
Then a grand pattern emerged.
How? We still don't quite know.
It sure is fun
To figure out how everything had begun
And God became One.
Then He ignited our Sun
And the Grand Pattern came to be.
Then He separated the land from the sea.
In the final phase
Emerged the human race.

To Sir Paul

Sir Paul,

I must confess

That I like you the best

Because you are the most fun.

From your early days

With your charming ways,

You certainly know how to

Keep your band on the run.

You say money can't buy love.

This may be wise,

But you can't keep love alive

If you don't have enough to survive.

It's a shame you couldn't

Get the boys back together

Before it was too late.

As a group or going solo,

The Fab Four will always be great.

Up and Down

The sky is up,
And the ground is down.
While the stock market is rallying up,
Bond prices go down.
When the sun first comes up,
The moon slowly drifts down.
When an elevator goes up,
It eventually must come down.
When a rocket goes up into space,
We pray
For the astronauts' safe return.
Whenever I board a plane,
I plan to soar above the clouds
And hope for a soft landing.
Whenever the quarterback makes a pass,
The football goes up
While the players scramble for a touchdown.
If you want to give God a loan,
Throw your quarters up high.
Keep the change.

An Interview with a Space Man

Show me the universe, both far and wide.
I want to know about the feelings
That you keep deep inside
That the media and government try to hide.

Mr. Spaceman, you may think of me as a hairy beast.
I hope you're not planning to abduct me,
To have me for a family feast.
Perhaps, you might offer something out of Star Trek
Which I might not be ready for
That could turn my home-life into a wreck.
Or, how about a clever toy
Which we could give to the kids.
The problem is
That this might make parents flip their lids.

Mr. Space Man, do you live very far away?
How long did it take you to get here—
Several years, or just a single day?
Did you bring your young ones along?
Can my kids dial them up and sing them a song?

Mr. Space Man, do you carry money?
I'd like to sell you something

Even if your currency is funny.
What souvenir would you like from earth?.
Does it matter to you how much it is worth.
Which would you prefer
A diamond or a few pennies?
Would you like a music CD
And a player to match?
Who would prefer to listen to,
The Beatles or Johnny Cash?
Mr. Spaceman, how did you learn
To speak earthly tongues?
Did you follow reruns
Broadcast to our young.

Mr. Spaceman,
Was there ever a Star Wars?
Does deep space follow different physical laws?
Do you have any lessons you want to teach us?
Will you ever talk to the public
When you finally openly greet us?
Will you always be a mystery?
Only viewed on cable TV?
Do you intend to be our enemy or friend?
Can we trust you in our hour of need
When faced with the possibility of earth's end?

Do you have humans like us
Stranded among you
Who long to come home?
How many years

Have they spent all alone?
Is their fame in you society
Or is everyone equal?
Will the real Star Wars
Ever have a sequel?

Mr. Spaceman, do your people believe in love?
Or are you matched by superiors above?
Have you mastered overcoming
International distrust and hate?
Will peace come to our galaxy,
Not a moment too late?

Mr. Spaceman, do you believe that individual destiny
Can be charted with the stars?
Do you worship a Supreme
Being Who is no different than ours?
Does your faith guide you
When danger requires follow-through?
If so, are you thankful and give praise
And walk away stronger in future days?

Ode to the
Grim Reaper

Grim Reaper, Oh Grim Reaper,
Don't come knocking at my door.
You see I've got plans
To live better and achieve more.
Don't you realize that I'm not through!
I've got places to go and things to do.

Grim Reaper, Oh Grim Reaper,
Please stay away.
Haven't I've been good?
Don't I deserve another day?

Later is better than sooner!
So bring your chilly darkness
To some other home.
You see I don't want to leave this world
Incomplete and all alone.
Wipe away your sarcastic grin.
I am well aware that eventually, you'll win.

Poetry Behind Bars

The steel bars are cold.
The concrete floor is gray.
I write poetry behind bars
To pass the time away.

If you write to me.
I'll be your pen pal.
Send me cigarettes and stamps
And that would be swell.

I need a woman with a kind heart
Who wouldn't mind being apart.

It's a bum-rap! I couldn't hurt a fly!
When I was booked,I told the Chief,
"You've got the wrong guy!"

While I may not end up
With benefits or a pension,
I'm looking for a shot at redemption.

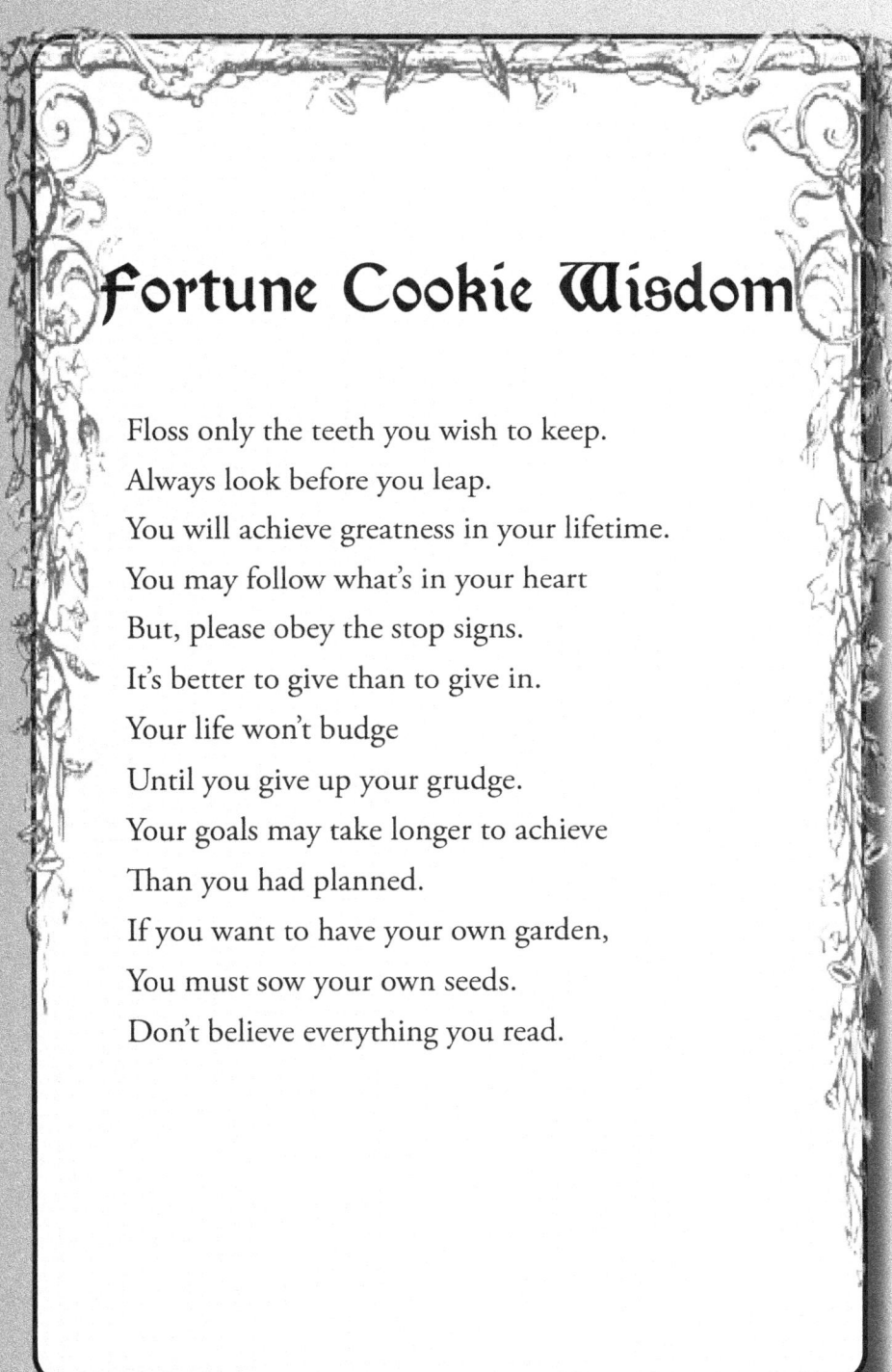

Fortune Cookie Wisdom

Floss only the teeth you wish to keep.

Always look before you leap.

You will achieve greatness in your lifetime.

You may follow what's in your heart

But, please obey the stop signs.

It's better to give than to give in.

Your life won't budge

Until you give up your grudge.

Your goals may take longer to achieve

Than you had planned.

If you want to have your own garden,

You must sow your own seeds.

Don't believe everything you read.

www.ingramcontent.com/pod-product-compliance
Lightning Source LLC
Chambersburg PA
CBHW051243120626
46547CB00014B/1767